The Guide to Google Places

*Get Your Local Business On The Map
and Let Your Prospects Find You!*

Kevin Wichtendahl

"Business has only two functions - marketing and innovation." Milan Kundera - Czech Novelist, Playwright and Poet, b.1929

Dedicated to Tom Pauley, Joe Vitale and Tim Ferris for showing me what was possible with a warped imagination.

Table of Contents

Introduction

I can picture this scene liked it happened yesterday. I was driving down one of the many back roads in Iowa. At a corner of a blacktop and gravel road there was a hand painted sign that said "Christmas Trees for Sale!" and had a red arrow that was pointing down the gravel road.

It immediately hit me as hilarious and I remember thinking to myself – "There is how most businesses are doing marketing today".

I followed that sign and stopped and asked him how business was. He told me he gets a lot of repeat business from previous year families, but customers are tough to get. In fact most new customers are from referrals.

As far as the sign goes it is actually the perfect message. The business is telling you that he has Christmas trees for sale. The problem is this: the only way the sign works is if the someone happens to be driving that direction; driving during daylight hours when the sign is visible; and the person driving down that road actually wants to buy a Christmas tree.

Does this describe your marketing efforts? Have you put a For Sale sign on a gravel road in the middle of nowhere hoping your prospects will see the sign?

The great baseball pitcher Wee Willie Keeler once said "Hit it where they ain't". I see many local business owners using the same marketing strategy of "Advertise where they ain't"

It is time to start advertising where they are!

As a business owner, you may have been hearing about this internet thing called Google Places. There's a lot of buzz about it but you may not really know what it is or why you should worry about it.

In this book, you will learn:

- The Yellow Pages Are Dead

- Some internet history that has led to the creation of Google Places

- What Google Places is

- Why you should be concerned about using Google Places

- What the benefits and features are that Google Places offers to you

- How to claim your Google Places listing

- Secrets that will explode your ranking in the search engines

The Yellow Pages Are Dead!

I am sorry if you are a sales representative that earns a living from the Yellow Pages, but if you are then it is time to find a new career (you can contact us – we might be hiring).

How can I proclaim the death of the Yellow Pages? See how many of the following questions / statements describe you:

- You just paid your Yellow Pages sales representative a 5-figure check for a fantastic ad in this year's Yellow Page book. They gave you a great deal on a full color, full page, most beautiful ad you have ever seen. 30 days after the printing of the Yellow Pages one of these things happened to your business:

  - Your lease gets cancelled and you have to move

  - Your business doubles and you have to move into new space

- You decide to implement a new telephone number

- You launch a new product or service

- You stop selling a new product or service

- You decide to offer a discount or special promotion on your service

- And so on...

Quick – call your Yellow Page sales representative and tell them what needs to be changed in your Yellow Pages ad and have them reprint and redistribute the Yellow Pages to every man, woman and child in your service area. What do you mean they won't do it? Who is running your business – them or you?

Or perhaps you should look at your own personal behavior:

- You are driving home one evening and you get a flat tire and you need a tow service. All you need to do is turn around, reach into your back seat, pull out your copy of the Yellow Pages and look up tow truck service or tire repair and give them a call.

- Tell your Yellow Pages representative that you only want to be charged for your ad if and when someone reads it and calls you based on that ad

- When you are at work or play, which is closer to you - a computer connected to the internet or a copy of the latest Yellow Pages?

This list could go on and on, but I think you are seeing the point. If you are marketing your business with Yellow Pages then you are not reaching the majority of potential customers who are searching for you.

I would argue that a savvy internet marketer could return as much as 10 times the ROI with an internet marketing campaign as your Yellow Pages ad.

This leads to yet another major drawback of Yellow Page advertising, radio advertising or any print advertising. How can you effectively measure the ROI of any of these old school methods? About the only way to do so is to have a special phone number listed in the ad for tracking purposes. But why would any business want to advertise multiple phone numbers for their place of business?

If you do not have a website, then your business could be on the same death march as the Yellow Pages. A few years ago some internet experts suggested that you should use both the Yellow Pages and an internet web strategy for your business. That was during the transitional period of the internet and before the advent of Smart Phones such as the iPhone, Droid, Blackberry, etc.

In today's world, the Yellow Pages can represent the worst investment a business could make. While there are some industries that can still benefit from Yellow Page advertising – those industries are getting fewer and harder to find.

The only thing that compares to this bad investment is television advertising, but that topic is for another book.

The Internet: Changing the Way Consumers Find Local Businesses

In the beginning, the internet was used primarily to connect people, to share information and to improve communication – all in a global sense. As internet use became more prevalent, big businesses realized the potential the internet gave them for reaching a global customer base and they embraced the internet with a vengeance.

Before long, every major corporation had an online presence and the impact this had on a company's growth in sales and customer acquisition could not be ignored by other businesses. With millions of people on the web every day, and the internet now a trillion dollar industry, it would be foolish not to try and harness this new technology to your advantage, no matter the size of your business.

Smaller business owners used to think that the internet could only be used properly by those large companies with huge advertising budgets. In the year 2000, millions of dollars were spent on both online advertising and offline advertising by companies trying to drive people to their company websites.

Well, we're very happy to report to you that this has changed and it is now possible for *you* to market *your business* on the internet and compete with those giant companies – using a much smaller marketing budget.

The Playing Field Has Been Leveled

The internet has been instrumental in leveling the playing field and allowing small businesses to compete with larger corporations, **using the right strategies**.

Over time, it's been found that people use the internet to research a product or a service. After they've learned about the product or service they want, those same customers are looking on the internet again – only this time to find a **local business** where they can buy that product or use that service.

Right now, people are looking on the internet for **your** local services and products instead of using the Yellow Pages phone book or newspapers. **If they're not finding your business** when they search, *you have a problem*! **Your competitors are getting your customers and your profit!**

You already know having an internet presence is important. You've probably even gotten a website made for your business.

But now what do you do with it?

And does your business get found by those local consumers using the internet, looking for your product or service?

Being Findable Online

Searches done on the internet are typically done on search engines, such as Google, Yahoo or Bing. It's generally acknowledged that Google is the most popular search engine, being used by about 65-70% of searchers. It would make sense, therefore, to pay attention to Google and learn how to be found on Google.

Here are some interesting statistics about search engines that you may not know:

- 43% of all searches on Google are related to searches for local services or businesses – (comScore Networks).

- 97% of consumers use the Internet to find and research products or services in their local area - (The Kelsey Group).

- 82% of people performing an online local search follow-up via an online inquiry, phone call or visit to an offline local business. This means these searchers decide which local business to spend their money at by the businesses they find on the Internet - (Local Marketing Source).

- 90% of consumer purchases are made within 20 miles of where they consumer lives.

- 75% of all auto purchases made in 2009 started on the internet – (JD Power & Associates).

Google, the largest collector of data, recognized the upward trending of local searches and made the decision to place an increased focus on local searches.

As a result, Google created **Google Places** – a strategy for giving searchers what they're looking for in their own local towns or cities - whether it is a restaurant, dry cleaner or attorney.

When you do an online search, Google will show local results first from local businesses, along with a map at the top of the page. Google Places listings are among those local results.

If you learn to optimize your Google Places properly and can be found by local consumers, you've won a major battle and can look forward to a profitable future as your business grows with online visibility.

Businesses that can get one of the top Google Places spots have a jumpstart on their competition.

The bottom line is...
If you're not findable online, you have competitors that are – and they're being found by your potential customers.

Local Internet Searches

Initially, people would use short "keywords" when looking for a website relevant to their needs. People would type things like "Furniture" into a search engine, check out the first few results and then make a decision. The difficulty with this was that the results would usually be global and not relevant enough.

Consumers now know that by adding geographical terms, such as city name, zip code etc... the search results provided will include local businesses.

In addition, since consumers are better at searching with Google, their keywords progressively became longer in order to return more specific, relevant results.

For example, instead of just "New York Furniture," they might type "New York discount office furniture." This would eliminate useless results such as, "home furnishing stores." These longer keywords are called "long tail keywords" and will result in more relevant search results.

This sort of mentality has revitalized the world of small businesses online. Instead of just searching for a product or service, people now search for a niche product or service in a particular location.

When people search in this way, **they are ready to buy**. This means that, instead of just massive chains dominating the search results, **local small business listings are flourishing**.

Why You Need an Optimized Google Places Listing

Being findable by local consumers online is known as **Local Internet Marketing** and requires a great deal of experience and expertise. Without applying Local Internet Marketing for your business, you won't be able to get your business findable online when local customers search for your product or service.

With more people moving towards local searches, you're going to need to target your Internet Marketing to services, product offerings and areas. If you fail to do this, you'll be competing with the major players in your industry nationally, and it's a battle you almost certainly won't win.

Google Places is the future of local consumer marketing - In fact, it's the "now" of local consumer marketing.

If you want to grow your business, you absolutely have to take advantage of this trend. Google has again confirmed, as they have over and over again for the last five years, that local search results are only going to get more important over time.

In October of 2010 Google made a major changes to their search results you may have noticed. Wherever relevant they will now show the map results on top of the search results. In fact, Google is now showing the map results OVER the paid listings.

Google is now also starting to Geo-Code the search results. What does this mean to you? Lets say that you are in Des Moines looking for coffee and you go to Google and type the word coffee. Not only will they show your coffee shop on the map at the top of the results (if you have an optimized listing), but they are also showing Des Moines coffee related sites in the organic search results on the first page of results.

By capitalizing on these changes you'll be able to get a strong foothold in your local marketplace.

Be Found - Get More Customers – isn't that the goal?

A Google Places listing allows you to show up on the first page of Google quicker than traditional SEO methods do. More customers finding your local business in a few weeks is much better than a few months or years.

With Google Places, your local business is easier for customers to find when you have an optimized Google Places listing. If you're not involved with Places, you're missing the boat on a very wide, very social demographic.

A growing number of consumers are looking at reviews of restaurants, business hours, locations, telephone numbers, and ideas about where to visit on their next trip or vacation, reviews of doctors, mechanics, schools, and countless other bits of information from Google searches.

"Google it" has become synonymous with performing an internet search. What's more – if you're not included, then you're overlooked.

Fortunately, driving traffic to your business has never been more attainable. Getting included on all of these search results can be as hands-on as you'd like.

You can submit your site yourself with minimal effort, often with less-than-optimal results, or you can **hire an Internet Marketing Expert** that knows the ins and outs of getting your business featured on search engines.

Stand Out.

Google Places' FREE services are quickly replacing the expensive ads local businesses have been paying for in the paper phone directories. **Local consumers are using Google Search more than ever.**

Your website, physical address, and your phone number are displayed **FREE** for your business, allowing new customers to find you quickly and sending you more traffic!

You are able to add photos, videos, hours of operation, and much more information to show customers what makes your business different – for FREE.

Get Insights.

Google provides you with a personalized dashboard where you can access data on number of visitors, popular keywords and where people traveled from to visit your business. You can use this information to make future decisions to make your marketing more effective.

Geo-Tagging and SmartPhone use

This is a growing market around the world. According to a report released in November of 2010, mobile Web traffic is expected to

29

increase by 700% over the next five years.

In fact, at this time, 86% of all mobile data usage comes from Internet-ready SmartPhones.

Nielsen projections show SmartPhone use overtaking all other phones by 2011 Q3, when they will achieve 51% market penetration.

Geo-Tagging, the use of SmartPhones to send location information along with data, is more widely accepted than one might believe.

Google tracks the locations of millions of phones while they deliver search results, and this allows your business to market to home PC users as well as SmartPhone users who are walking down the Avenue that your business occupies.

Customized QR codes:

From the dashboard page of Google Places, businesses in the U.S. can download a QR code that's unique to their business, directly from their dashboard page.

QR codes can be placed on business cards or other marketing materials, and customers can scan them with certain SmartPhones to be taken directly to the mobile version of the Place Page for that business.

Beating your competitors to the punch is the goal of any marketing effort. Right now, in most areas, local internet marketing efforts are applied inefficiently or are completely ignored.

So What Does All This Mean?

With just a small marketing budget and/or a bit of work, you have an opportunity to become findable when local consumers are looking for your product or service.

Unlike other Internet marketing strategies which your competitors may have caught on to, (such as a website with strong Search Engine Optimization techniques), right now, emerging strategies like Local Search Marketing are relatively uncompetitive and more affordable.

By taking advantage of this untapped opportunity, **your marketing budget can go much further than with traditional marketing alone**. Google has had a history of rewarding early adopters.

Until your competitors adopt a local search marketing campaign, not only will you be listed on the first page of Google, you might also be the primary listing in your area, and net all the traffic.

The bottom line is: **if you're findable on the internet** – you're more likely to get more customers and this translates into **more profits for your business**.

YOU NEED A Google Places Listing !

Keep reading and we'll show you how to claim your own Google Places listing.

Information You Need For Your Listing

Company/Organization Name

It's important to list your business just as it is anywhere else that you advertise. Your real business name as you would list it in the phonebook.

If Google detects a discrepancy between your business name, your Website, other online advertising and Google Places listings, you could potentially be penalized. Hiring a Local Internet Marketing Expert can help you avoid being penalized for errors in your listings.

Friendly Chevrolet
www.friendlychevy.com/

  2754 N Stemmons Freeway, Dallas · (214) 920-1
"Overall, this was a great experience and I will def
my next car here." - dealerrater.com (10)
judysbook.com (4) - citysearch.com (2) - yelp.con

John Eagle Honda
www.eaglehonda.com/

  5311 Lemmon Avenue, Dallas · (888) 246-0744
"Pros: Honest, fair, painless ... Cons: none come
went to this store in ..." - edmunds.com (12)
dealerrater.com (98) - citysearch.com (21) -
insiderpages.com (11)

In this example, Friendly Chevrolet is the real business name of this car dealership. Both of these businesses are showing only their real business.

Business Address and Website Address

Your business address is very important. You HAVE to be very consistent with your address when creating listings. Google looks for discrepancies when it sees your address on your listings, your website and other internet sources and you would not want your account to get suspended (just a possibility).

If you are a business where the client always comes to you to do business, then you are going to want to list your storefront address. If you are in a business where you go to your customers' houses or workplaces or if you work from home, Google allows you to hide your address.

Google has also implemented a "Service Area" feature that allows you to designate a service area radius, up to 60 miles or 100 kilometers, or list specific cities/towns you want to target.

East **Texas Tyler** Kia Volkswagen **Dealer** | Crown Motor Company
New ... ☆

Tyler's local Kia Volkswagen **dealership** for new cars, used cars, auto parts, finance and service. Get a hassle free new or used **car** quote .
www.crownkiatx.com/ - Cached

 4818 Troup Highway, Tyler
(903) 581-7688
insiderpages.com (3)

☆☆
6 re·
Place

Phone Number

You'll want to use a local phone number instead of an out-of-state or toll free number. You want your customers (and Google) to recognize the number as a local number they can trust.

Description

Including a strong description is necessary for achieving a high ranking in Google Places. Your description is the first thing Google Places looks at to see who you are and what you do. It's *also the first place that potential customers look to see if you offer the goods and services they're looking for.*

An appropriate, keyword-rich, well-targeted description is necessary for ensuring the success of your marketing results. You want to use as much of the 200 characters allowed when writing your description. Make sure you always write for humans while including the most important search terms for your business.

This is where a marketing consultant can help you understand how to optimize your listing. Selecting keywords with high search traffic is something that a marketing consultant knows how to do.

Category

Picking the right category is really a task for a marketing professional, which is why a consultant is critical if you want this listing to be optimized. Google checks categories to make sure that they're consistent with the content on your Website and the keywords in your Google Places description.

Far too much goes into selecting categories (you can have up to five) to discuss in this guide, but I will mention the most important information that an industry professional would consider before selecting a category for your Google Places listing.

- The first category that you choose should be one of Google's categories. As you start typing your category, you'll see a drop down list of possible categories. You must select one of these for your primary category if you hope to rank highly in Google Places.

- Your other four categories should ideally be categories in Google's category list, but this is not a requirement. You should create your own category only if you think Google would approve, or if they have approved similar categories in the past. You can always change this later.

- Google will look at the five categories in the order that you place them. The most important category goes at the top, and the least important category goes in the fifth slot. This is a vital decision to ensure you're ranked highly for terms that users search for. The decisions you make will depend on your marketing goals.

Becoming highly visible for keywords you care about...

Is becoming more critical by the day. If you use Google Search, you'll notice the Google Search Results feature a map prominently on the right side of the page.

The map lists several businesses that are near the city you live in or the city you searched for.

Your goal is to become one of the top businesses through proper optimization of your Google Places listing, because front page ranking in the search engines can translate into more customers finding you.

Being findable online is critical for creating increased traffic to your business, and one of the ways you can achieve it is through an optimized Google Places listing.

How to Add Your Business to Google Places

Here are some basic steps to follow if you want to add your local business to Google Places:

- If you don't already have one, you'll need to create a Google Gmail account. Go to http://www.google.com/gmail and then click on "Create an account." Remember, this is for a business account so you won't want to use your personal email address.

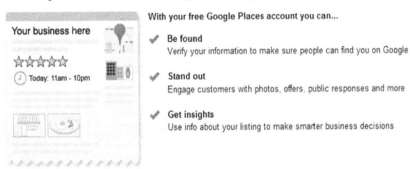

Google places

Claim your business listing on Google. It's free!

Your business here

☆☆☆☆☆

Today: 11am - 10pm

With your free Google Places account you can...

✔ **Be found**
Verify your information to make sure people can find you on Google

✔ **Stand out**
Engage customers with photos, offers, public responses and more

✔ **Get insights**
Use info about your listing to make smarter business decisions

---

- Go to the following URL:
  http://www.google.com/places & login using
  your Gmail username & password. Click
  on "Add a New Business" as shown below.

- Select your Country and enter your local
  business phone number. Then select "Find
  business information". Your business may

44

already be on Google Maps, but if it isn't, then click the button that says, "Add a new listing."

Google places

Tip: Before you create a business listing, think about which Google Account you a

Enter your business's main phone number to see if Google Maps already has some details, including photos and videos. About Google Places

Country   United States   ▼

Phone number

ex: ▥ ▼ (201) 234-5678 🌐

Find business information »

▼ Basic Information

Please note that changing your address or business name will require additional verification via mail or phone.

Country: *   United States   ▼

Company/Organization: *

Street Address: *

City/Town: *

State: *   Select state   ▼

ZIP: * [?]

Main phone: *

                   Example: (201) 234-5678 Add more phone numbers

Email address:

                   Example: myname@example.com

Website:

                   Example: http://www.example.com
                   ☐ I don't have a website

Description:

200 characters max, 200 characters left

- Enter your basic information such as Business Name, Address, Phone Number, Email Address, Website & Category.

- Add the optional informatio n like business hours, photos, videos, payment options and service areas to your listing too.

Not only does Google use these additional details about your business to rank your listing higher, it also provides valuable information for your customers.

WARNING: In the description of your business or the keywords section, do NOT list the city or service area you serve. This may sound a bit strange, but Google

46

Places matches your business description and keywords with the search location where the search is originating.

Google knows where the search is being originated from based on the IP address of the service provider you are connecting from. If you are sitting in West Des Moines Iowa and do a Google search for "barber", Google will show the search results for barbers in West Des Moines Iowa. If you are in New York City and search for barbers, you will not see barbers located in West Des Moines.

If you include your city name or service area in your Google Places listing, as of May 2011, Google may view this as spamming and rank your site lower than other sites that do not do this.

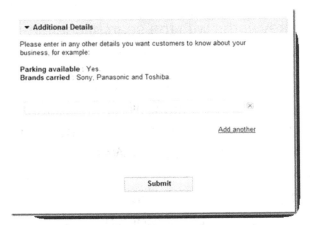

▼ Additional Details

Please enter in any other details you want customers to know about your business, for example:

Parking available : Yes.
Brands carried : Sony, Panasonic and Toshiba.

Add another

Submit

Secret Tip:

In the above Additional details box,

How would you like to validate your listing?
For your protection, we need to verify the information you've just given us. This can be done in one of 2 ways:

○ **By phone**
We'll call you at this phone number

○ **By postcard (2-3 weeks)**
We'll send you a postcard in the mail to this address

Houston TX 77042
United States

If necessary, you may specify another recipient or enter a mailstop/mailbox number below. *This information won't appear on Google Maps.*

Contact name:

By clicking 'Finish,' you're authorizing Google to create or update your business listing for use in Google Maps or other Google services. You are also affirming that you have the right to create this listing and that you have read and agree to Google's terms of service. There is currently no charge for creating or displaying listings. If this is a new listing or has a new address, you must verify the address via regular mail or telephone before the listing is activated. See next page for instructions.

Finish

this is generally used for product information, but we can use for some much more. It is hard to tell from the picture from above, the left and right columns are required. For example, in the left column you would type Brands carried, and in the right box you would type the type of brands you carried.

However, we can use this for so much more. You should use this box to link to some of the reviews about your business. Here are some powerful examples:

Left Column: See Our Facebook page

Right Column: www.facebook.com/you

Left Column: Check Out Our BBB rating

Right Column: www.bbb.com/yourpage

Left Column: Read Yelp Reviews

Right Column: www.yelp.com/yourreview

Use your imagination to link any important information to direct your prospective clients to important information that will help create trust.

- After you fill in this information, click "Submit" which will take you to the validation step.

- Validate your listing. You will need to validate your listing in order to show Google that you own or control the site you are listing. At this step they will have you confirm the address and contact that a postcard will be sent to. It usually takes only 5 days for the postcard from Google to reach you.

  Prior to 2011, Google gave you the option of receiving an automated verification phone call, but they removed this option in May of 2011.

- PIN number. Google will either give you the PIN on the postcard. This PIN number will activate your listing. If you do not receive this activation post card within 5 days, you can logon again and request a new one.

  Please note this postcard is a standard white postcard and is very easy to throw away. You should let whoever handles

your mail to be on the lookout from a
postcard from Google.

Status ↓

Needs Action
⚠ Not yet published ⑦
  Enter your PIN: [   ] [Go]

Request another PIN

Google Places Offers & Reviews

Offers and Coupons

Another key element of Google Places is the Offers section. Filling out an offer can drive tremendous amounts of traffic to your front door. Google likes to see you fill out the offers and keep the information updated and relevant.

For every user who walks through your front door, coupon in hand, you have a customer likely to purchase. Customers can either print the coupon offers or use a mobile coupon.

With mobile coupons, customers find your offer in your Google Places listing and show you the coupon on their mobile phone to get the discount without printing it out.

Google places

Mobile

 Show this coupon on your phone at the participating business.

New York Discount Furniture
Free Delivery

No Charge next day delivery with any furniture purchase. Bedroom, Dining Room or Living Room Suites. You can have it in your house tomorrow.

Expires - **Dec 31, 2011**

Reviews

Getting your company reviewed on Google Places will also improve your business' chances of ranking well. Some businesses have hundreds of reviews on Google. If you really want new customers to show up at your business, get several hundred positive reviews on Google.

Here are some ideas for soliciting reviews from your customers.

- **Call your best customers and ask.**

- **Append the request to e-mail newsletters.**

- **Ask for a review during follow-up calls.**

- **Review the results of a satisfaction survey, and e-mail a review request to happy customers.**

The Ideal Google Places Listing

Searching in some of the most competitive markets in the world, you can see some of the greatest Google Places listings on the planet. Those listings were probably written by **Internet marketing professionals**. They use all of the techniques that we have discussed in this guide.

Examples of good Google Places listings are shown below. You should try to emulate them when formulating your own listings. Be sure to take advantage of everything Google Places allows you to share with

Las Vegas Hotels - Bellagio

Bellagio is ultimate **Las Vegas hotel** experience. Make your luxury hotel reservations at the home of the famous dancing fountains, award-winning casino. ...
www.bellagio.com/ - Cached - Similar

3600 South Las Vegas Boulevard, Las Vegas -
(888) 987-6667
"Overall, we enjoyed our stay at Bellagio very
much and would definetly go
back!" - tripadvisor.com (3596)
diningguide.com (20) - holidaycheck.de (18) -
travelandleisure.com (13)

☆☆☆☆☆
3759 reviews
Place page

The Venetian - Resort, **Hotel, Casino** ☆

Of the top hotels Las Vegas offers, The Venetian **Las Vegas Hotel** Casino sets new luxury standards: Suites twice the size of other Las Vegas suites
www.venetian.com/ - Cached - Similar

3355 South Las Vegas Boulevard, Las Vegas,
Nevada - (702) 414-1000
"Overall, the Venetian is a great place to stay. The
location is super as well." - tripadvisor.com (2658)
priceline.com (265) - insiderpages.com (31) -
hotels.com (24)

☆☆☆☆☆
3221 reviews
Place page

Treasure Island **Hotel & Casino** ☆

Guests looking for excellent **Las Vegas hotel** room rates and **Las Vegas hotel** deals will definitely want to book a room at TI **hotel** casino with the ideal ...
www.treasureisland.com/

3300 Las Vegas Boulevard South, Las Vegas -
(702) 894-7111
"Overall would stay again. The bargain price was
outstanding for a strip hotel." - igougo.com (53)
tripadvisor.com (2323) - priceline.com (162) -
holidaycheck.de (18)

☆☆☆☆☆
2731 reviews
Place page

Hotel Mirage ☆

Things to do in **Las Vegas** - The Mirage. Escape to the exotic - a world tantalizing to the imagination and the senses. The Mirage. **Vegas** Starts Here. What's New
www.mirage.com/

3400 Las Vegas Boulevard South, Las Vegas -
(702) 791-7111
"Overall it was a nice room and if you can get a
good deal online it is worth
it." - tripadvisor.com (1978)
booking.com (47) - priceline.com (34) -
holidaycheck.de (16)

☆☆☆☆☆
2310 reviews
Place page

potential customers.

The Secret To A Top Google Places Ranking

There is one additional step to getting a high Google Places Ranking that is rarely openly discussed.

Ideally, you should finish this step before creating your Google Places listing. If you have already created your Google Places listing, you still need to implement this strategy, but it may take a few extra weeks to see these powerful results.

A Friend of My Friend Is Also My Friend

Before we begin this secret step, which in many ways is the most important step of all, we need to define some terms:

Google Algorithm: The Google algorithm is proprietary and has undergone many changes since the inception of Google. Basically this algorithm is what determines where your website shows up in the Google search engine results. In late 2010, when Google decided to put a lot of emphasis on local search, they applied this same type of algorithm to local search results.

Page Rank: Google assigns your website a number from 0 to 10 based on their algorithm. Zero is the lowest, 10 is the highest. Google's own site ranks a 10. ESPN and CNN rank a 9. New sites will either be unranked or a zero.

There are many tools and browser add-ons that will show you what your page rank is currently. The easiest is to use the Google search tool / add-on that is available for free from Google and works with all browsers. Within the settings of the Google toolbar, you will see a tab called Privacy. When you click that, go to the bottom of the screen where it says Enhanced Features. Make sure there is a checkmark next to Use PageRank to see Google's importance of a page. With this checked, you will now see a green bar on the top of the page. When you hover your mouse pointer over this green bar, it will display a number. This is your PageRank.

Please note that Google only updates your sites' pagerank every 90 days, so there is no need to check it daily.

Authority Site: An Authority Site is a site with a higher page rank than yours. If your site has a PageRank of 1 and my site has a PageRank of 4, then my site is considered an Authority Site when compared to yours and I have a link from my site to yours.

Inbound Link: This is a link from another site to yours. Do not get this one wrong. Links from your site to other sites are called Outbound links. You should not focus on Outbound links. Only focus on getting Inbound links to your site.

Now that we have these termed defined, we can put all of these together and put this strategy into place.

While the actual Google algorithm is one of the most safeguarded secrets in the Internet world, there are several things about it that we know from a lot of testing and trial and error. Through this testing it has been discovered that one of the most important things you can do in order to get your business to show up on the top of the

Google Places results is by use of Inbound linking.

The use of proper Inbound linking is perhaps the single most important thing you can do to in order to get your site listed at the top of the local search results is to obtain in-bound links from authority sites.

The best way to understand this is to visualize this. If your site has a pagerank of zero and you obtain an inbound link from a website with a pagerank of 2, then you have an inbound authority link. Think of the Google pagerank as a reflection of trust. Google "trusts" the judgment of higher-ranking sites more than they "trust" sites with lower PageRanks.

How to Obtain Good Inbound links from Authority Sites

One of the easiest and most powerful ways to get inbound links from authority sites is from review sites. Google has placed a high trust on review sites and these are very easy to get inbound links from in order to boost your site in the search results.

The first site you should always list your site on is SuperPages.com. Google seems to put a lot of trust into SuperPages.com because SuperPages.com also verifies your business address.

The other sites where you need to have your site listed are:

- Yelp.com

- YouTube (see instructions below)

- Insider Pages

- Merchant Circle (free listing only)

- Local.com

- BBB.com, if available

YouTube Listing

This simple strategy is too often ignored by local businesses. You probably already know that Google owns YouTube. It stands to reason that Google would think sites listed within YouTube would also be pretty important sites.

Getting a video advertising your local business on YouTube is very easy. The first thing you need to do is create a very short video to put on YouTube. Potential topics for this video include:

- You, speaking directly into a video camera or web cam talking directly to a potential customer and explaining to them why they should do business with you. Remember that people buy from people and making them feel comfortable with you before they call can ensure a sale.

- A video of your product in action

- A slideshow of some pictures of your place of business with some background music playing. I have even seen clients who have a 30 second recording of a 1-page slide that just gives their business contact information.

Please note that the main reason we are doing a YouTube video is for the link building. If it is a quality video that also brings customers into your door then that is a bonus.

When you submit your video to YouTube, you are given a description box to describe the video. Here is where and how we place the link and business information.

In the Video Description box, you should enter something similar to this:

Information on our house painting services in Dayton Iowa. We have been painting homes is Dayton Iowa since 1988.

You can learn more at http://www.yoursite.com

123 Main Street

Your Town, ST, 50000

Of all of the information above, the most crucial is your full website address (including the http://)

Also not the keywords we placed in the video description. Within YouTube you can and should list your location information and important keywords. By doing this, your video has a very good chance of coming up on page 1 of Google search for your keywords. In this example above, the video should show up to people searching for "house painting Dayton Iowa". Much cheaper than any television commercial and much more targeted.

Please note that if you need assistance in creating or submitting your video, please contact us at Kevin@desmoinesseo.com for a quote.

Ethical Link Building

Many customers have asked if it acceptable for them to write their own reviews on these sites in order to obtain these powerful links. This is a decision you will have to make for yourself. A very common view is this: If you have actual customer reviews that customers have written you or told you about in person, then all you are doing is recording their own words on their behalf.

Please be aware that if you do this, you will need to be intelligent about this practice since is a violation of these sites to write your own reviews. You will need to create a separate email address for this purpose and it is also very advisable you do this review work from a separate computer.

There is very little use in obtaining inbound links from sites that have a PageRank of zero. Make sure you are getting inbound links from Authority Sites, as defined above.

Being Found On The Internet

People use the internet in very different ways, and you can't possibly hope to capture every single person who might be looking for a product or service like yours. However, you can make it extremely easy for people to find your business by being prominent in multiple places online.

With so many different types of content, and various ways of receiving information, there are limitless possibilities for marketing your website on the internet. Whether in the form of local business directories, online classifieds or videos about your product posted on popular websites, the opportunities for local consumers to find your business are endless.

Internet marketing is essentially about being "found" online by the people who will become your customers. They are looking for what you are selling, and you have to make it as easy as possible for them to find you.

Your business should be listed all over the internet: in classifieds, directories, videos, search engines, and, of course, Google Places. Once this has been done, there will be a flood of eager customers wanting to do business with you.

An Internet Marketing Consultant is familiar with all these strategies and will be happy to help you market your business for optimum results.

One Tool Out of Many

My father had a saying he used a lot. It was "Use the right tool for the right job". This saying holds true whether you are fixing a plumbing problem or marketing your business to the world. Some of these tools include:

- Facebook. Facebook traffic now exceeds Google in terms of total visitors each day. Did you know you could advertise your business or service on Facebook and in some cases for free?

- Pay Per Click. Imagine only paying someone when a prospect actually visits your website.

- Mobile Adverting. Your business ad can now appear on any Smart Phone for only the service area you wish to target. This area of marketing is in its infancy. The good news is that ad prices are ridiculously low for now. I have seen examples of 2000% ROI using Mobile Advertising. If your product or service matches up well to this target demographic you could be missing out on a gold mine.

- Email marketing. Spam is evil; Permission based email is great. Spam has received so much negative press a lot of businesses have stayed away from this type of marketing all together. This is unfortunate because those that understand permission based marketing are dominating their markets.

- Video. Online video is a must on the web. The most important part of making a sale is making a personal connection with your prospect. Which creates a stronger connection – the prospect reading your website, or you taking 30 seconds to explain to the prospect what your business or service can do for them?

Benefits of hiring a professional

Hiring a Local Internet Marketing Expert to provide valuable services is extremely important in competitive markets when it comes to being findable in multiple places when consumers are looking for your product or service online.

After all, you do visit a lawyer for legal advice, and you see a doctor for illnesses, so use a Local Internet Marketing Expert for your internet marketing needs.

Make a decision today

Your competitors are certainly learning about the new Google Places. You have to beat your competitors to the punch if you want to really succeed in marketing. This is your chance.

More Help?

I hope that you have found this book to be helpful. If you follow the simple steps listed, you should be able to create and claim your 1st page Google listing in a very short period if time.

If you need any assistance, we do offer consulting and listing services for a select number of clients. For more information you can contact us at Kevin@DesMoinesSEO.com

More Findable = More Customers = More Profits!